Facts of Life - Pippo Lionni

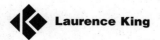

Facts of Life are visual – there is no sound

I lie awake nights trying to pull the Facts of Life out of my ceiling. Sometimes they are good and I can build on them, they mean something, they come to life and fly on their own – the others are dead-enders. It's hard to recognize the good ones before wasting time on the duds. Making an almost self-evident image is very difficult. There is no method, the process isn't rational – I just do it until it either works or I get fed up. The list of image-resistant ideas is endless.

Facts of Life as a language is open ended, unorganized and structureless. It is ambiguous, imprecise and impartial. Each symbol is intentionally created to lack descriptive detail, thus to avoid codifying reality. They are non-linear indivisible wholes to be read from any direction and in any order. There are no prescribed meanings – there are only catalysts to provoke interpretation. In a classroom a 6-year-old kid found that Sisyphus on the move had more power and freedom than Atlas static under his globe.

Facts of Life is not optimistic or pessimistic. It is critical, even brutal at times. There is no invention of an aesthetic – I want Facts of Life to be anti-style, to be non-decoration. If, as images, they are beautiful it is not intentional.

Pictograms are supposed to be self-evident. This is the perversion of comfortable stereotype

understanding. They use what is "without a doubt" to produce doubt, the "universal" to talk about specificity, what is simplistic and dead to talk about life, and what is abstract to emancipate the personal "I" from the generalized "man" – falling man is really dancing!

The language is very basic, it is archetypal and just a bit more elaborate than what one might find on signs in any international airport or bus station. And those signs are in themselves sometimes very confusing. One often finds the symbol for toilet (man separated from woman by a vertical line) next to the one for elevator (man and woman in a box). Neither of these symbols is self evident, thus they are not pictograms but rather ideograms (images that must be learned). The image for toilet is in itself very interesting. It is almost impossible to put the image of a toilet on a sign – it just is not acceptable. In its place one finds a man, or a woman or both. The symbol for toilet is thus person. We are toilets, toilets are we, and the most important thing about the toilet place is that it's for women or men or men and women separated by a wall.

The captions included at the bottom of each page are intentionally vague. Their purpose is to help people to invent their own interpretations rather than to provide a key to decipher or to explain. The truth is in you – find it.

Pippo Lionni, 17/10/00

to defy

obsession and ...

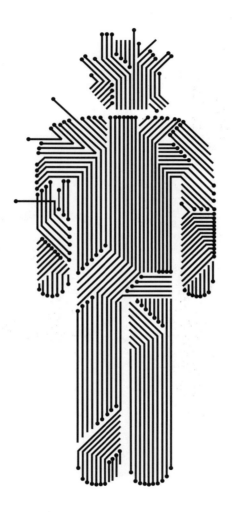

printed circuit man 13

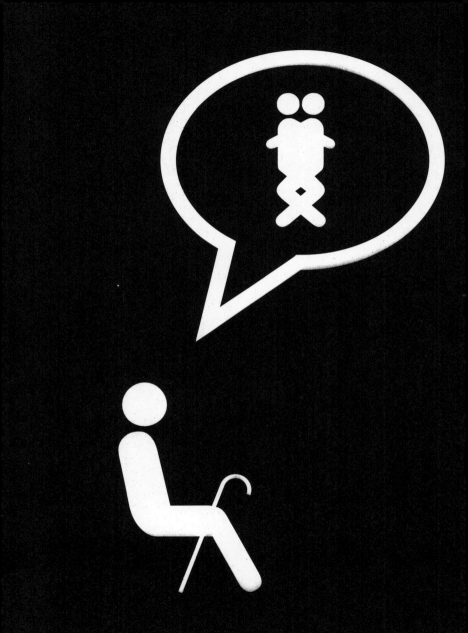

the gift . . .

interpretations

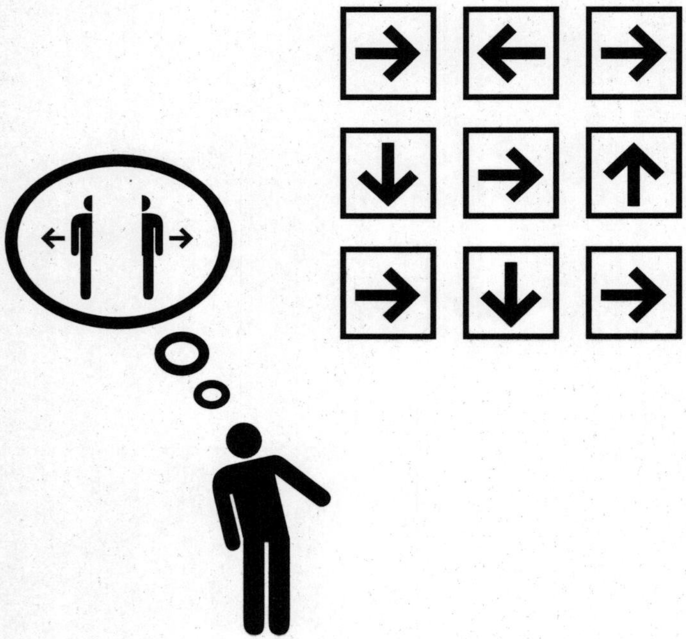

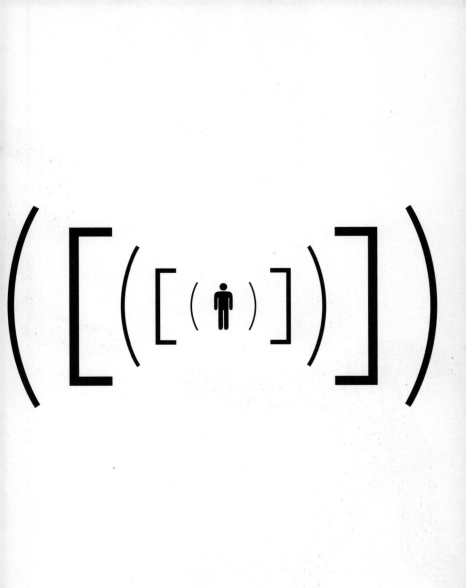

up against the wall

throwing heads

4, 2, 3 and 4 point contact

mind over matter

human as tube

flip

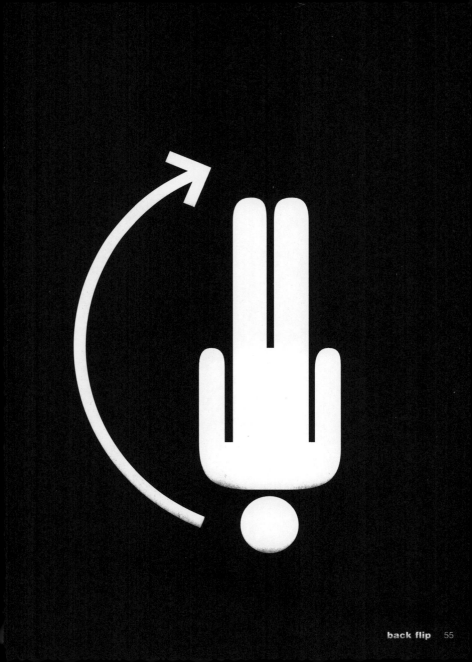

protected

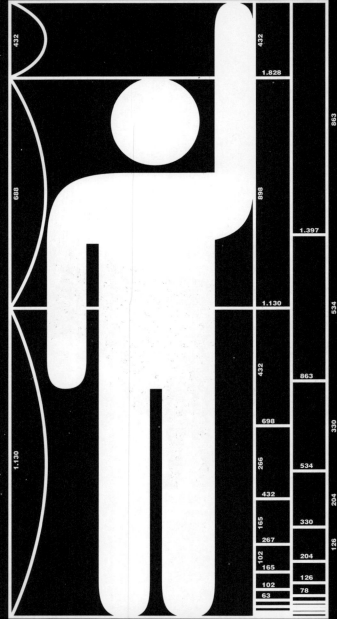

machine man

tension

reality is . . .

0.792"

1.528"

0.148"

4.639"   3.042"

0.806"

136.835°

1.563"   3.570"

82.147°

3.483"

4.131"

48.417°

1.553"   2.482"

370"

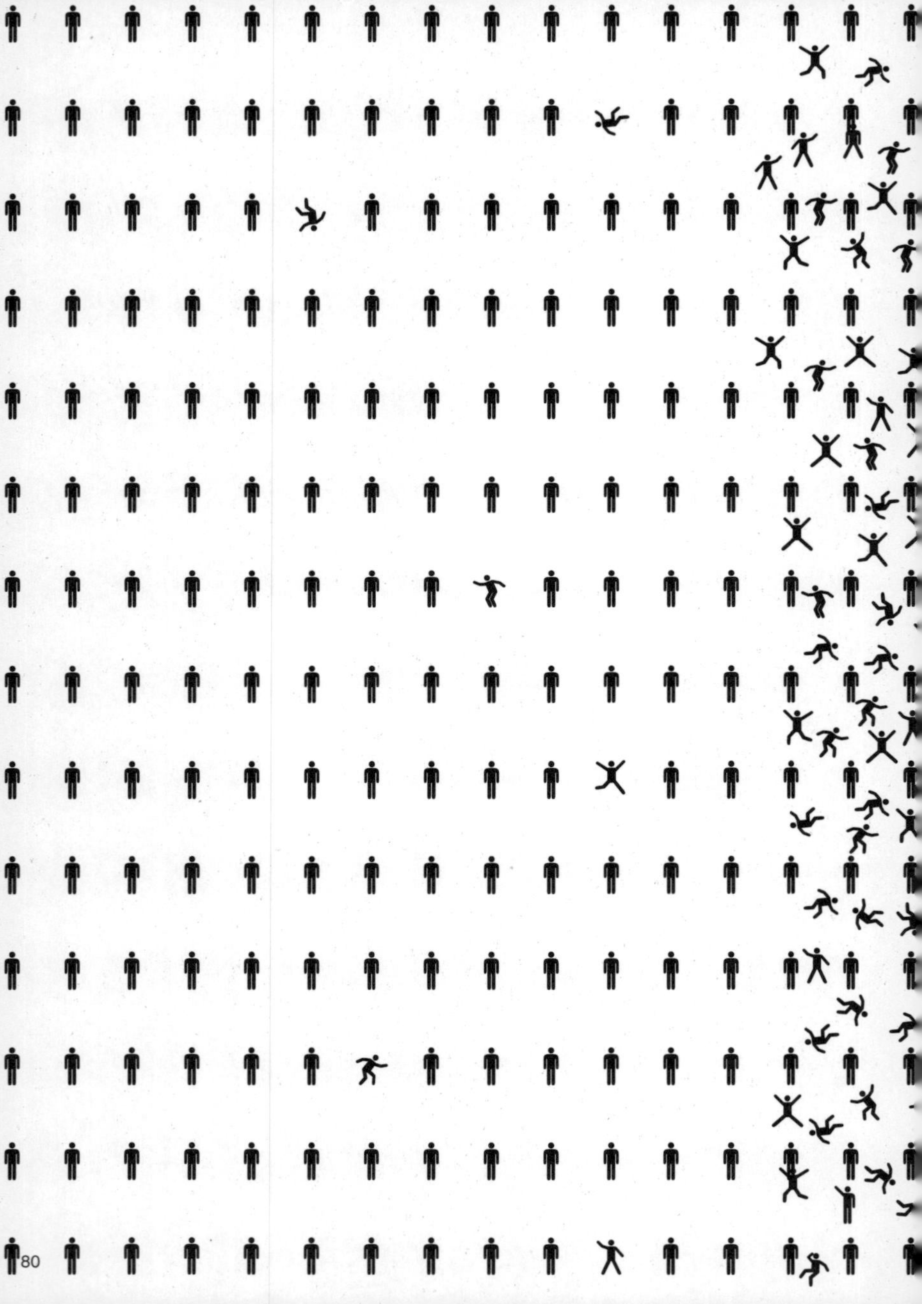

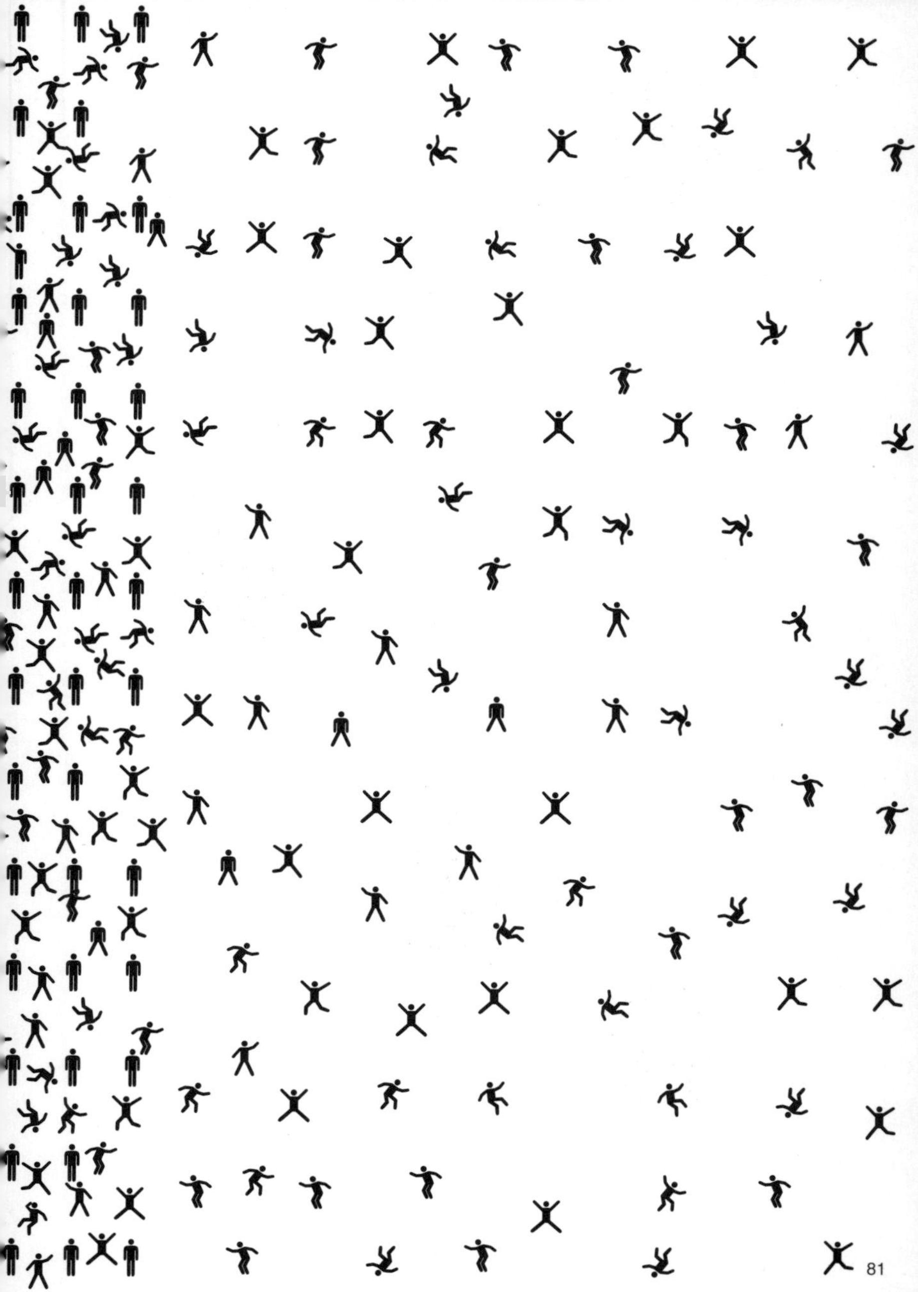

$$\sqrt{\{\text{👤👤👤}\}}\,\chi\,\gamma + \sqrt{\text{👤}}\,\pi + \sqrt{\text{👤👤}}$$

$$\sqrt{\{\text{👤👤👤}\}} + \sqrt{\text{👤}}\,\pi + \sqrt{\text{👤👤👤}}$$

$$\sqrt{\{\text{👤👤👤} \pm \text{👤👤👤}\}} \doteqdot \sqrt{\text{👤}}\,\pi$$

$$\sqrt[\beta]{\{\text{👤👤👤}\}} + \sqrt[\alpha]{\text{👤}} + \sqrt{\text{👤👤👤👤}}$$

$$\sqrt{\{\text{👤👤👤} \pm \text{👤👤👤}\}} \doteqdot \sqrt{\text{👤}}\,\pi$$

$$\overline{\text{🚹🚹}} \neq \{\text{🚹}+\text{🚹}\}''''\,\pi + \{\text{🚹}+\text{🚹}\}\,\chi\gamma$$

$$\neq \{\text{🚹}+\text{🚹}\}''''\,\pi$$

$$\sqrt{\text{🚹} \pm \{\text{🚹}\,\text{🚹}\,\text{🚹}\}} \doteqdot \text{🚺}\,\pi$$

$$\alpha\{\text{🚹}+\text{🚹}\}'''' + \beta\{\text{🚹}+\text{🚹}\}''$$

$$\pm\sqrt{\text{🚹} \pm \{\text{🚹}\,\text{🚹}\,\text{🚹}\}} \doteqdot \text{🚺}\,\pi$$

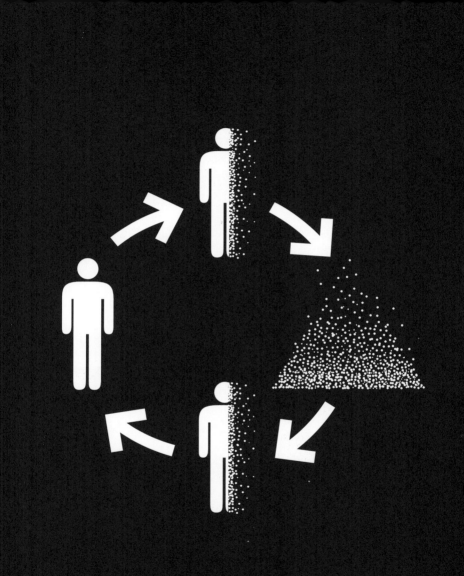

danger from above

word pollution

for french sailors only

8310335448378

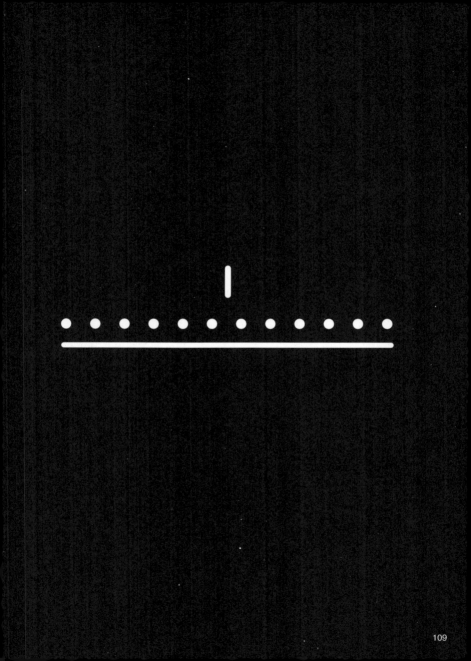

24.55 KM/H

the media is the message

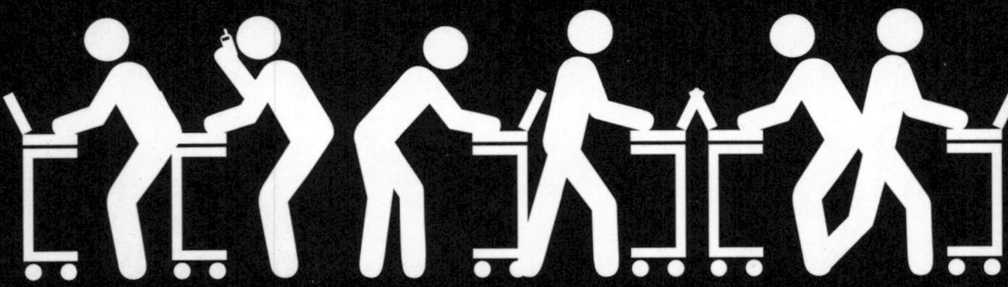

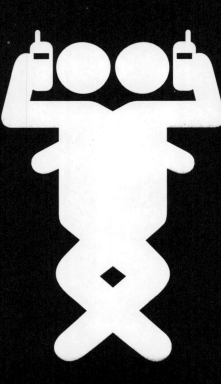

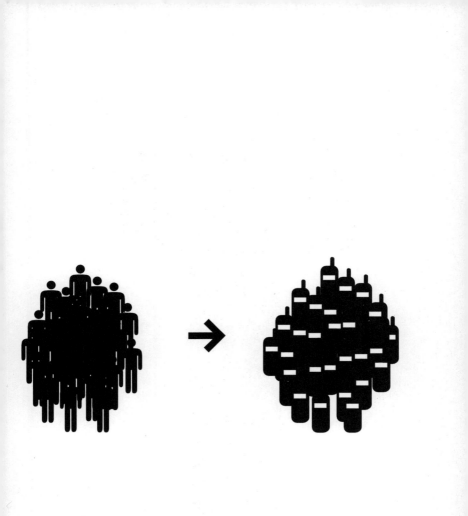

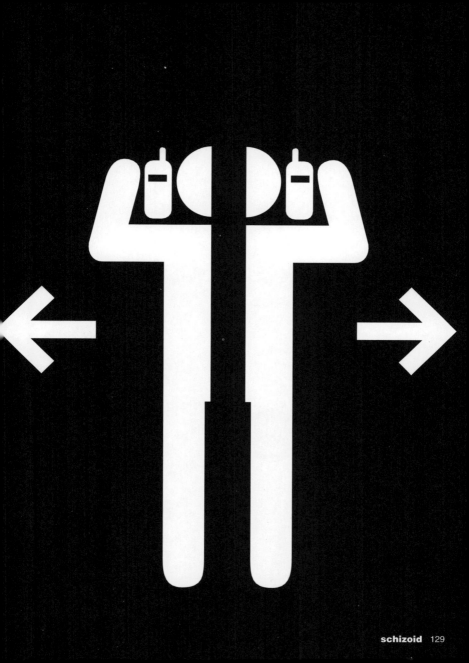

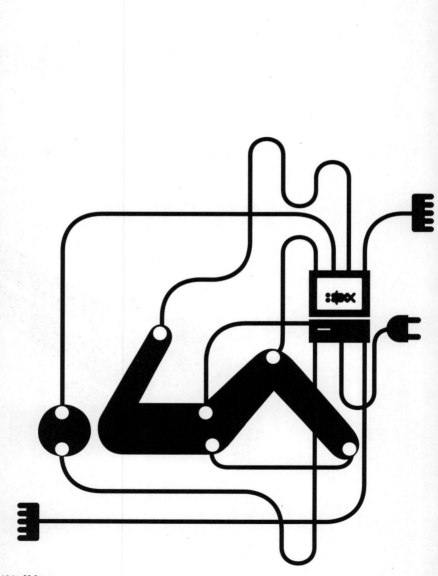

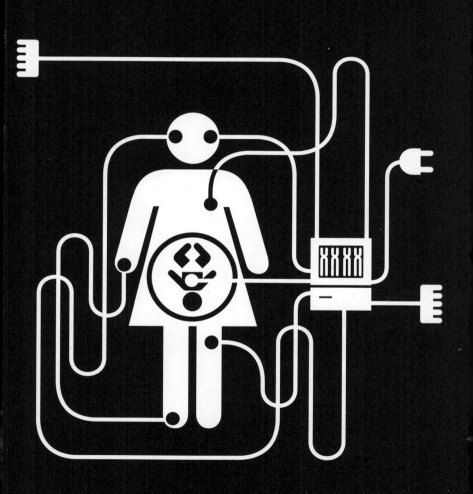

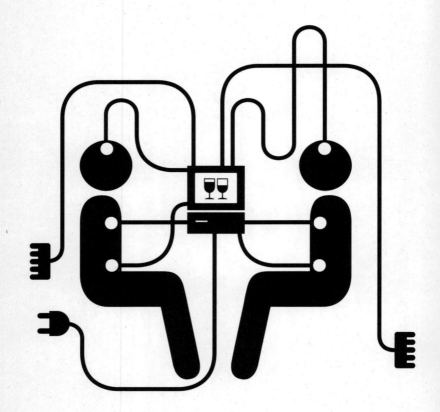

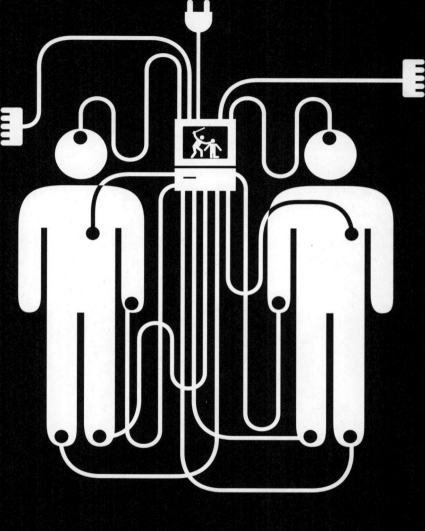

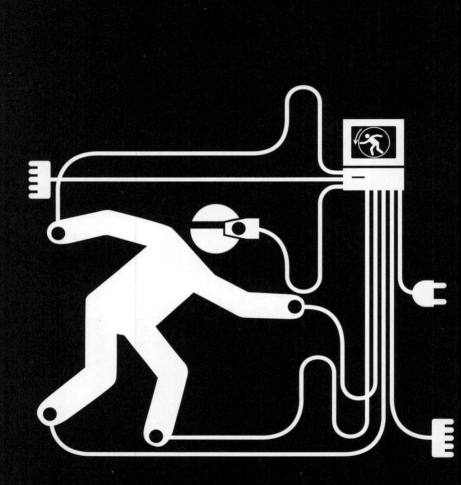

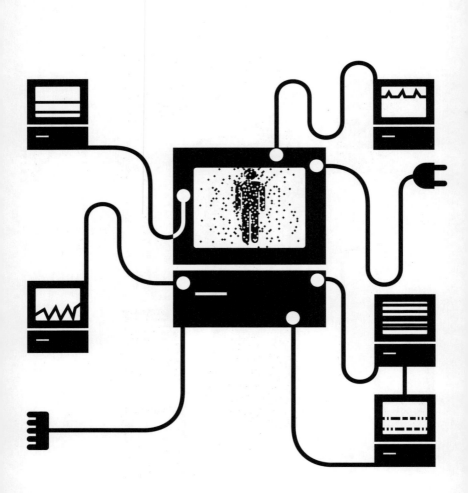

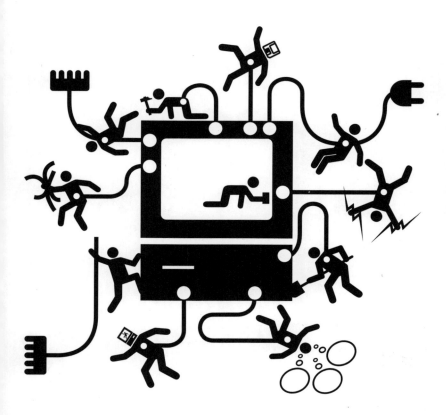

Pippo Lionni grew up in a New York family of architects, escaped into Philosophy and Mathematics at Portland State University and New York University, played jazz in New York and Paris, and became a designer in the late 1970s. His offices and partnerships: Design Pippo Lionni (1984-89), Integral Concept (1989-95), Pippo Lionni et associés (1995-97), and Ⓛ**design** in Paris bring to design a conceptual approach of diversified influences as formalized in complex multidimentional systems, such as signage, scenography, corporate identity programs, environmental design.
In 1998, Pippo Lionni began work on Facts of Life - a symbolic language to question our most profound perceptions with a laugh. First presented at Typomedia 98 in Frankfurt, Facts of Life 1 was published in a first edition in 1999. Facts of Life images have been produced as a font by Linotype (Volume 498, for Apple Macintosh and PC), on bags by Viahero, as beach towels by Move, and as postcards by Nouvelles Images. In 1999, Revolution of the Species – 7 dayglow pictograms on 2 x 1.2 meter galvanized steel sheets – was presented in the group show at Le Passage de Retz.

a special thanks to
Stéphanie Chavanon, Edouard Bonnefoy.

© Idea and copyright of all artwork by **Pippo Lionni**

Published in 2001 by Laurence King Publishing
an imprint of
Calmann & King Ltd
71 Great Russell Street
London WC1B 3BP
Tel: +44 020 7430 8850
Fax: +44 020 7430 8880
e-mail: enquiries@calmann-king.co.uk
www.laurence-king.com

Copyright © 2001 Verlag Hermann Schmidt Mainz

A catalogue record for this book is available from the British Library.

ISBN 1 85669 256 6

Printed in Germany